Joke Books

by Judy A. Winter

**Consulting Editor:** Gail Saunders-Smith, PhD

CAPSTONE PRESS
a capstone imprint

Pebble Books are published by Capstone Press,
151 Good Counsel Drive, P.O. Box 669, Mankato, Minnesota 56002.
www.capstonepub.com

Books published by Capstone Press are manufactured with paper
containing at least 10 percent post-consumer waste.

*Library of Congress Cataloging-in-Publication Data*
Winter, Judy A., 1952–
  Knock-knock jokes / by Judy A. Winter.
    p. cm.—(Pebble Books. Joke books)
  Includes bibliographical references.
  Summary: "Simple text and photographs present knock-knock jokes"—Provided
by publisher.
  ISBN 978-1-4296-4468-6 (library binding)
  1. Knock-knock jokes. 2. Wit and humor, Juvenile.  I. Title. II. Series.
  PN6231.K55W56 2011
  818'.602—dc22
                                                                    2010002783

**Editorial Credits**

Gillia Olson, editor; Ted Williams, designer; Sarah Schuette, studio specialist;
Marcy Morin, studio scheduler; Eric Manske, production specialist

**Photo Credits**

All photos by Capstone Studio: Karon Dubke except: Capstone Press: Gary Sundermeyer,
14; iStockphoto: Johan Swanepoel, 6 (elephant); Shutterstock: Gary Blakeley, cover, 22
(tank), Milos Luzanin, cover, 22 (flag), trucic, background (throughout)

## Note to Parents and Teachers

The Joke Books set supports English language arts standards related
to reading a wide range of print for personal fulfillment. Early readers
may need assistance to read some of the words and to use the Table of
Contents, Read More, and Internet Sites sections of this book.

Printed in the United States of America in North Mankato, Minnesota.
122010        006032R

# Table of Contents

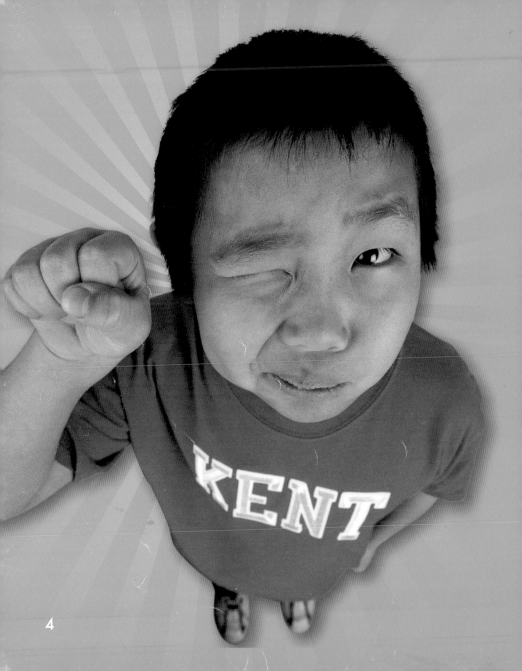

Knock knock.

**Who's there?**

Kent.

**Kent who?**

Kent you let me in?

Knock knock.

**Who's there?**

Les.

**Les who?**

Les go to the zoo!

Knock knock.

**Who's there?**
Alma.

**Alma who?**
Alma candy is gone!

Knock knock.

**Who's there?**
Sarah.

**Sarah who?**
Sarah mouse in
your house?

Knock knock.

**Who's there?**
Aardvark.

**Aardvark who?**
Aardvark a million miles to see you.

Knock knock.

**Who's there?**
Pig.

**Pig who?**
Pig up your feet
or you might trip.

Knock knock.

**Who's there?**

Butter.

**Butter who?**

Butter watch your dog!

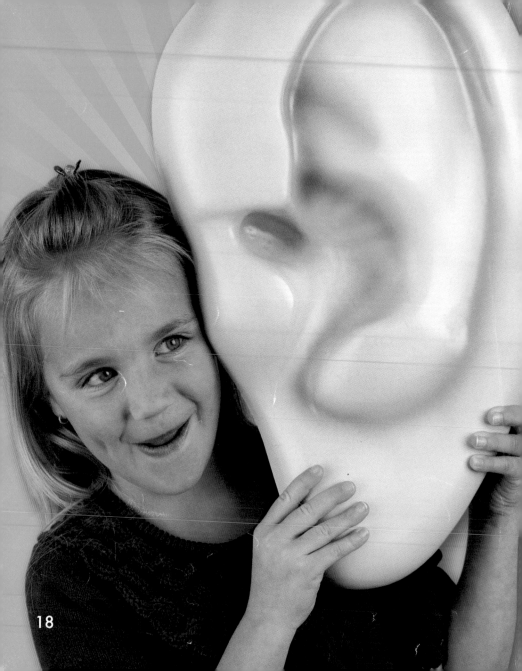

Knock knock.

**Who's there?**
Ears.

**Ears who?**
Ears some more knock-knock jokes for you.

Knock knock.

**Who's there?**
Woo.

**Woo who?**
You don't need to cheer. It's just a joke.

Welcome

Knock knock.

**Who's there?**
Tank.

**Tank who?**
You are welcome.

# Read More

**Dahl, Michael.** *Open Up and Laugh!: A Book of Knock-Knock Jokes.* Read-It! Joke Books. Minneapolis: Picture Window Books, 2004.

**Freymann, Saxton, et al.** *Knock, Knock!* New York: Dial Books for Young Readers, *2007.*

**Phillips, Bob.** *Good Clean Knock-Knock Jokes for Kids.* Eugene, Ore.: Harvest House, 2007.

# Internet Sites

FactHound offers a safe, fun way to find Internet sites related to this book. All of the sites on FactHound have been researched by our staff.

Here's all you do:

Visit *www.facthound.com*

Type in this code: 9781429644686

Word Count: 127          Grade: 1
Early-Intervention Level: 20